Time for Korean

Book 1

Time for Korean

Book 1

Second Revised Edition

Inshil Choe Yoon
with contributions from Sun Hee Kim and Jung Hee Lee

Basic Korean for Young Learners

Hollym

Carlsbad, CA and Seoul

This work was supported by the Korea Research Foundation Grant
(KRF-2002-038-00-C-05) and the Embassy of the Republic of Korea in New Zealand.

Time for Korean (Book 1)
Basic Korean for Young Learners

Originally published as "Beginner's Korean 나미, 안녕?"
© 2002 by Inshil Choe Yoon
Second revised edition, 2019
by Hollym International Corp., Carlsbad, CA, USA
Phone 760 814 9880
http://www.hollym.com   **e-Mail** contact@hollym.com

 Hollym

Published simultaneously in Korea
by Hollym Corp., Publishers, Seoul, Korea
Phone +82 2 734 5087   **Fax** +82 2 730 5149
http://www.hollym.co.kr   **e-Mail** hollym@hollym.co.kr

ISBN: 978-1-56591-188-8
Library of Congress Control Number: 2006926994

Printed in Korea

Contents

Preface

During the last two decades Korean language programs have been introduced in secondary and primary schools in the United States of America, Australia and New Zealand. While the number and the backgrounds of students learning in the schools vary, one of the common difficulties in teaching the Korean language seems to be acquiring resources that suit the needs of both students and teachers. This book has been developed to cover some of the urgent needs in Korean language teaching at primary and intermediate schools in New Zealand and in other English-speaking countries.

This book is the first of two textbooks of the Korean language designed for beginners at upper primary and intermediate school levels. Based on a communicative approach, this book aims at fostering students' skills of listening and speaking Korean through various stimulating activities as well as learning relevant aspects of Korean culture. This book attempts to provide students with an opportunity to explore basic reading and writing skills which can consolidate the acquired oral/aural proficiency. The ten units in the book can be covered over a term if Korean is taught for two periods a week; if taught for one period a week, this book can be used over two terms. The units are divided into small sections so that part of a unit can be used for a shorter teaching period, and yet still provide a useful lesson.

Each unit consists of either two or three sets of a dialog and an oral task, classroom instructions, songs or chants, role-play, word checking, culture note, the Korean alphabet and a review. They are task-oriented and integrated for step-by-step Korean language learning with relevant audio input from audio files. Romanization of the Korean alphabet is provided in oral tasks and in other sections. It is advised, however, to listen to the audio files for accurate pronunciation of Korean words. Games, inserted after every three units, are fun and further enrich the Korean language learning experience in the classroom.

The structure of each unit is as follows:

Look and Listen is a contextualized and minimal unit dialog. It is followed by Let's Talk, an oral task. After acquiring the pattern of the conversation through aural and visual aids, students are encouraged to make their own dialog related to their class situation.

Each dialog and oral task set is followed by one or more relevant activities such as Let's Move, Let's Sing, Let's Chant and Let's Role-play. These activities are designed to enhance students' listening and speaking skills further.

Culture note is designed not only to introduce students to Korean culture but also to provide them with activities related to aspects of Korean culture.

Listen and Check, with its aural and visual presentation, provides students with an opportunity to check important phrases or words in each unit.

Let's Learn the Korean Alphabet introduces a small number of the letters of the Korean alphabet at a time—letters which are used in the dialogs. It also provides opportunities of reading words solely made up of these letters and those already learned. This Korean alphabet section will make learning the Korean alphabet an easy, step-by-step and meaningful exercise in the context.

Let's Review, made up of oral and written tasks based on the dialogs, provides learners with further opportunity for review.

In addition, Let's Play a Game, inserted after every three lessons, is designed to offer a fun activity that will further enrich the spoken language learning experience. At the end of the book, Checklist is provided to aid students in self-monitoring. Answers and List of Words and Phrases will also aid them for their self-assessment and active language use.

Many tasks and challenges lie ahead in developing Korean language programs in secondary and primary schools. I sincerely hope that this book and its audio files will contribute to the enhancement of Korean language programs everywhere.

Acknowledgments

Many people helped me in the development and publication of this textbook. My most sincere gratitude goes to Dr. Sun Hee Kim and Mrs. Jung Hee Lee for their fine work. Their experience, especially of teaching Korean language to students of this age, made a great contribution toward this book. They wrote the first draft on Korean culture and made an invaluable contribution in revising earlier stage drafts. Their contribution in the cultural notes and their comments in the initial preparation of this book are most appreciated.

I thank the Korea Research Foundation for their financial support in the development of this book. I would also like to thank the Embassy of the Republic of Korea in New Zealand for their sponsorship toward the publication. I would like to thank the teachers of the Korean language in intermediate schools in New Zealand, especially Mrs. Pauline Dick and Mrs. Cherlie Gurney for their involvement in assessing the practicality of draft lessons, their feedback and suggestions, as well as Mrs. Rosa Lee, Mrs. Eun-hee Kim and Mrs. In-hee Lee for their comments. My gratitude goes to Mr. Chol-nam Chon for his advice on publication and for proofreading the final layout of the book, to Mr. Ernie Warren for proofreading the manuscript, and to Mr. Chang-sub Kim, Mr. Sung-won Yoon and Mr. Seung-ryel Lee for their generous support.

I would also like to thank Jeanette McKerchar for recording and editing the audio files, Jae-hun Woo for the recorded dialogs and songs, So-hee Jeong, Yeon-hee Ji and James Koo for the songs, Lee Martelli and Helen Park for accompaniment, Mathew Langridge and Jae-hoon Kim for recording the songs and Marilyn Humphrey for her useful advice for producing the audio files. I am indebted to Mrs. Hee-kyoung Lee in Canberra for her valuable comments and Mrs. I.S. Kang in London, Mrs. Sook-hee McRoberts in Sydney and Ms. Dorothy Chung in Los Angeles for sending me related materials.

I am grateful to my parents and brothers. I thank Mrs. Jan Westwood, who helped me start the path of language teaching, and the Birkenhead Play Centre parents, who generously shared their lives in working with children. I thank all the colleagues in the School of Asian Studies of The University of Auckland, especially those with whom I have been teaching the Korean language and culture. Finally, I would like to thank ReneeMarie for her feedback, and Annabelle, Frances, Caroline, Albert and Hong-key for their encouragement and support.

Inshil Choe Yoon

안녕하세요?
Hello!/Hi!

Look and Listen 1

TR 02

••• Let's Talk

Greet the people around you as shown in the picture above.

"안녕하세요?"   "안녕하세요?"
annyeonghaseyo   annyeonghaseyo

TR 02

일어나세요.
ireonaseyo
Please stand up.

앉으세요.
anjeuseyo
Please sit down.

Let's Sing   "안녕하세요?"
annyeonghaseyo

♪ 안녕하세요?
annyeonghaseyo

안녕하세요?
annyeonghaseyo

안녕하세요?
annyeonghaseyo

안녕하세요?
annyeonghaseyo

Let's Sing with Actions

Two sets of partners (four students) make a circle. Singing the first line, greet your partner and bow in turn. Greet the others in the circle while you sing your part in the second line.

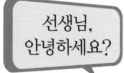

••• Let's Talk

Greet your teacher as shown in the picture above.

"선생님, 안녕하세요?"
seonsaengnim annyeonghaseyo

"안녕하세요?"
annyeonghaseyo

••• Let's Role-play

선생님, 안녕하세요?
seonsaengnim annyeonghaseyo

Some students can act as teachers.
Greet them with the "선생님" title.

Look and Listen 3

••• Let's Talk

Greet five people around you with their names as Ana and Ian do.

"이안, 안녕?"

ian annyeong

"아나, 안녕?"

ana annyeong

Listen and Check

Listen carefully to the following words.

1.	2.	3.	4.	5.
이안	선생님	아나	안녕하세요?	안녕?
ian	seonsaengnim	ana	annyeonghaseyo	annyeong

••• Let's Do It Match the picture with the word that is read out.

a. ☐   b. ☐   c. ☐   d. ☐   e. ☐

The Korean language has been spoken for thousands of years on the Korean peninsula, and is now spoken by over 78 million people around the world. It is the native language to more than 76 million people living in Korea and a heritage language to nearly seven million ethnic Koreans living in such countries as China, the United States, Japan, the former Soviet Union, Canada, Australia, Philippines, New Zealand, Britain, Germany, Brazil and Argentina. An increasing number of people are learning Korean as a second or foreign language in the above and other countries.

The Korean language is written in the Korean alphabet. King Sejong the Great (세종대왕 Sejong daewang) during the Joseon Dynasty(1392-1910) created this unique writing system in 1443 through scientific and systematic research and experiments. Because the Korean alphabet is so easy to learn, almost all Koreans living in Korea can read and write Korean.

The basic consonants of the Korean alphabet were modeled after the shapes of the organs where the sounds are produced. Three of the consonants are shown below:

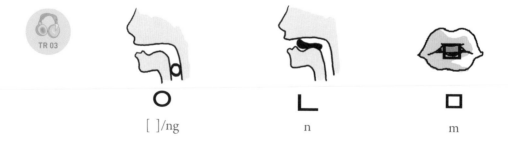

ㅇ [ ]/ng   ㄴ n   ㅁ m

Initially, the vowels were made up of three basic shapes representing the universe: • stands for heaven; — stands for the earth; │ stands for human beings.

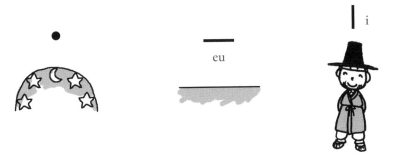

By combining or adding these shapes to each other, various shapes of vowels were made to represent the vowel sounds. For example, when • is added to the right hand side of │, it becomes ㅏ a (Koreans started using a short stroke in place of •). Today, 24 basic letters consisting of 14 consonants and 10 vowels are used.

Some Korean vowels with either │ or — as the starting point are shown below.

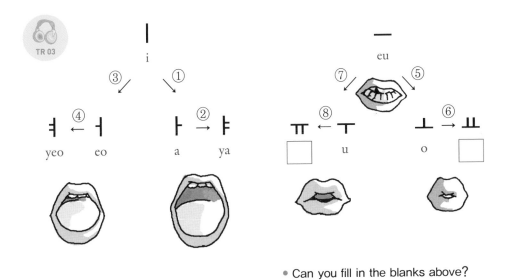

• Can you fill in the blanks above?

Let's Learn the Korean Alphabet

Consonants: O [ ]/ng ◎   ㄴ n

Letter	Order of Strokes	Practice				
O	⟋O					
ㄴ	ㄴ					

When the Korean consonant "ㅇ" comes at the beginning of a syllable, it does not carry any sound value. The general rule for writing Hangeul is from top to bottom and from left to right.

Vowels: ㅣ i   ㅏ a   ㅑ ya

Letter	Order of Strokes	Practice				
ㅣ	↓ ㅣ					
ㅏ	①↓ ㅏ②					
ㅑ	①↓ ㅑ②③					

••• Let's Read

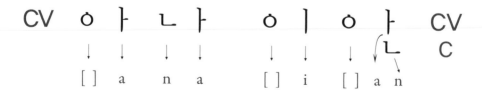

CV ㅇ ㅏ ㄴ ㅏ   ㅇ ㅣ ㅇ ㅑ CV
                                      C
  ↓ ↓ ↓ ↓   ↓ ↓ ↓ ㄴ
 [ ] a n a   [ ] i [ ] a n

* C stands for a consonant, and V stands for a vowel.

··· Let's Read More

 아이

 양

Let's Review

1. Say and act.

안녕하세요?

안 _____ ?

2. Link up the names.

1) 이안 ●   ● a) Ana

2) 아나 ●   ● b) Ian

3. Complete the crossword.

Across: Ian

Down: Hi!

이	
	녕

4. Fill in the blanks with Korean syllables from the box.

나 이 안

□안, 안녕?
ian annyeong

아□, □녕?
ana annyeong

만나서 반가워요.

Glad to meet you.

Look and Listen 1

TR 04

만나서
반가워요.

만나서
반가워요.

··· Let's Talk

Shake hands with five people around you, and say that you are glad to meet them as shown in the picture above.

"만나서 반가워요."
mannaseo bangawoyo

"만나서 반가워요."
mannaseo bangawoyo

Let's Move

TR 04

노래하세요.
noraehaseyo
Please sing.

춤추세요.
chumchuseyo
Please dance.

Look and Listen 2

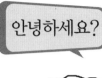 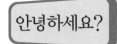 

••• Let's Talk

Greet three people around you. While shaking hands, say that you are glad to meet them as in the example above.

"안녕하세요?"
annyeonghaseyo

"안녕하세요?"
annyeonghaseyo

"만나서 반가워요."
mannaseo bangawoyo

"만나서 반가워요."
mannaseo bangawoyo

 TR 05

Let's Sing "만나서 반가워요."
mannaseo bangawoyo

 안녕하세요?
annyeonghaseyo

안녕하세요?
annyeonghaseyo

만나서 반가워요.
mannaseo bangawoyo

반가워요.
bangawoyo

 **Let's Sing with Actions** Work with your partner. While singing the song, shake hands with or bow to each other.

Look and Listen 3

⋯ Let's Talk

Say good-bye to three people and say that you will see him/her again as shown in the picture above.

"나미, 안녕! 또 만나요."
nami annyeong   tto mannayo

"어니, 안녕! 또 만나요."
eoni annyeong   tto mannayo

⋯ Let's Role-play

안녕! 또 만나요.
annyeong tto mannayo

A student is going toward the door. Say good-bye and say that you will see him/her again.

이안, 안녕! 또 만나요.

안녕! 또 만나요.

Listen and Check

Listen carefully to the following words.

1.
나미
nami

2.
어니
eoni

3.
만나서 반가워요.
mannaseo bangawoyo

4.
안녕! 또 만나요.
annyeong tto mannayo

⋯ Let's Do It Match the picture with the word that is read out.

a. ☐   b. ☐   c. ☐   d. ☐

한국 Korea

Hanguk

The Korean peninsula lies in the northeast of the Asian continent and is between China and Japan. About 70 percent of the land is mountainous and Koreans have long grown rice on the plains of the southern and western regions.

Korea has four distinctive seasons. Spring is March, April and May. It is warm and various flowers blossom all over the country. Summer lasts from June to early September and it is hot and humid. Temperatures can go beyond 30℃. People go to swimming pools and beaches to enjoy water sports. Autumn lasts from mid-September to November. It is the harvest season and the most pleasant time of the year. A lot of Koreans enjoy hiking in the nearby mountains which have colorful autumn leaves. Winter is December, January and February. It snows heavily in mountainous areas and temperatures often drop below -10℃.

Korea was one unified country for over a thousand years before it was divided into South and North Korea at the end of World War II. Over 51 million (2017) people live in South Korea and over 25 million (2016) in North Korea. The two Koreas suffered greatly during the Korean War (1950-1953). Recently, they have been working together in tourism at Mt. Geumgang, reconnecting railways between the two countries and developing and managing the industrial area around Gaeseong City.

Some Korean companies well-known to the world market include Samsung (mobile phones, computers, computer chips, TVs and refrigerators), Hyundai (cars and ships), LG (mobile phones, TVs and washing machines), SK (mobile services and computer chips) and KIA (cars). Many Korean companies make and export various electronic appliances and stationery products. We can easily find goods made in Korea in countries around the world.

• Do you know anything else that is made in Korea?

Let's Learn the Korean Alphabet

 Consonants: ㅁ m   ㅂ b

Letter	Order of Strokes	Practice				
ㅁ	①↓ ②□ ③→					
ㅂ	③→ ①↓ ㅂ ②④→↓					

Vowels: ㅓ eo   ㅕ yeo

Letter	Order of Strokes	Practice				
ㅓ	①→ ㅓ ↓②					
ㅕ	①→ ② ㅕ ↓③					

⋯ Let's Make shapes

Using your body as the main stem, move your arms so that you make the shape of the vowels which you have learned. Ask your partner to guess what they are.

⋯ Let's Read

나미　　어니　　안녕　　만나　　반

⋯ Let's Read More

 어머니　　 바나나　　 나비

Let's Review

1. Say and act.

만나서 반가워요.

만나서 _____ .

2. Link up the names.

1) 어니 ●   ● a) Ernie

2) 나미 ●   ● b) Nami

3. Complete the crossword.

Across: Meet

Down: Nami

4. Fill in the blanks with Korean syllables from the box.

반   만나   안녕

1) 나미: **만나서 반가워요.**
   mannaseo bangawoyo

어니: **만나서 ☐가워요.**
   mannaseo bangawoyo

2) 나미: **어니, 안녕!**
   eoni annyeong

나미: **또 만나요.**
   tto mannayo

어니: **나미, ☐☐!**
   nami annyeong

어니: **또 ☐☐요.**
   tto mannayo

Unit 03

보세요.
Please look.

Look and Listen 1

··· Let's Do It

Take turns with your partner, giving each other the above instructions.

"보세요."
boseyo

"들으세요."
deureuseyo

Let's Move

따라 하세요.
ttara haseyo
Please do as I do.

발 드세요.
bal deuseyo
Please lift up your foot.

••• Let's Do It

Repeat after your teacher with the appropriate gesture.

"말하세요."
malhaseyo

"조용히 하세요."
joyonghi haseyo

"손 드세요."
son deuseyo

"손 내리세요."
son naeriseyo

Let's Sing   "일어나세요."
ireonaseyo
TR 07

 일어나세요.(×2)
ireonaseyo

일어나세요.(×2)
ireonaseyo

보세요.(×2)
boseyo

손 드세요.(×2)
son deuseyo

들으세요.(×2)
deureuseyo

발 드세요.(×2)
bal deuseyo

앉으세요.(×2)
anjeuseyo

앉으세요.(×2)
anjeuseyo

학교　Schools

hakgyo

Children attend a kindergarten for one or two years before they enter elementary school. They start elementary school when they are eight years old. After attending elementary school, 초등학교 (chodeung hakgyo), for 6 years, children go to middle school, 중학교 (junghakgyo), for three years. They then go to high school, 고등학교 (godeung hakgyo), for three years. Students can choose to go to either general high schools or vocational high schools. Many students go to university, 대학교 (daehakgyo), which normally lasts for four years.

　　The schools in Korea start in March. During the first semester, schools have a day for a spring picnic to historical sites such as old palaces or parks. The first semester ends in the second half of July. The summer vacation lasts until the end of August. During the summer vacation, children enjoy swimming on beaches or riversides and camping. The second semester starts in the beginning of September. Students have a long winter vacation, which begin in the later part of December and continue through January and February.

- When do children in your country start school?
- For how many years do elementary school students attend school?

Listen and Check

TR 07

Listen carefully to the following words.

| 1. 보세요. | 2. 들으세요. | 3. 말하세요. | 4. 조용히 하세요. | 5. 손 드세요. |
| boseyo | deureuseyo | malhaseyo | joyonghi haseyo | son deuseyo |

··· **Let's Do It**　Match the picture with the word that is read out.

a. ☐　　b. ☐　　c. ☐　　d. ☐　　e. ☐

One student comes forward and mimes two of the following expressions.
The rest of the class has to guess what he/she is trying to say.

일어나세요.
ireonaseyo

 앉으세요.
anjeuseyo

보세요.
boseyo

들으세요.
deureuseyo

손 드세요.
son deuseyo

발 드세요.
bal deuseyo

말하세요.
malhaseyo

조용히 하세요.
joyonghi haseyo

Let's Learn the Korean Alphabet

Consonants: ㄷ d ㄹ r/l

Letter	Order of Strokes	Practice			
ㄷ	①→ ㄷ ②				
ㄹ	① ③ㄹ②				

When "ㄹ" comes at the final position of a syllable and a vowel does not follow it, it is pronounced [l].

Vowels: — eu ㅗ o ㅛ yo

Letter	Order of Strokes	Practice			
—	①→				
ㅗ	①↓ㅗ ②→				
ㅛ	①↓ㅛ↓② ③→				

••• Let's Read

C ㅂ b C ㄷ d 들으세요.
V ㅗ o V — eu 보세요.
        C ㄹ l 손 드세요.

••• Let's Read More

 돈 달 말 별 라디오 요요

Let's Review

1. Link the expression and its matching drawing.

1)

2)

3)

a) **보세요.**
boseyo

b) **들으세요.**
deureuseyo

c) **손 드세요.**
son deuseyo

d) **발 드세요.**
bal deuseyo

e) **말하세요.**
malhaseyo

f) **조용히 하세요.**
joyonghi haseyo

4)

5)

6)

2. Complete the crossword.

   Across: Please listen.

   Down: Please look.

3. Fill in the blanks with Korean syllables from the box.

들으   보   손   요

1) ☐세요.
boseyo

2) ☐☐세요.
deureuseyo

3) 손 드세☐.
son deuseyo

4) ☐ 내리세☐.
son naeriseyo

Let's Play a Game "안녕하세요?" Hello!/Hi!
annyeonghaseyo

■ **Aim:** To act out greetings and instructions

■ **Method:** Groups of two or three students get together with a playing piece for each player. A game of "Rock, paper and scissors" is played by saying "gawi, bawi, bo" to decide who starts the game for each round. The winner starts the conversation in space 1 and the others reply with appropriate actions. In each round "gawi, bawi, bo" is played and the winner moves the amount of spaces as in the table on the right page. For example, the person who wins a round with scissors (gawi) moves his/her playing piece one space; the person who wins the round with rock (bawi) moves two spaces; the person who wins the round with paper (bo) moves three spaces. Those who make a mistake go back one space. Whoever lands on space 3 or 4 must go to space 7 or 8, respectively, after they finish the given task(s). They also have to act out the tasks in space 7 or 8. The person who reaches the end first is the winner.

① 안녕하세요?

② 앉으세요. 일어나세요.

③ 안녕?

가세요 →

가세요 →

④ 보세요. 들으세요.

⑤ 선생님, 안녕하세요?

안녕! 또 만나요.

⑩

⑨

손 드세요.

발 드세요.

⑧

춤추세요.

노래하세요.

만나서 반가워요.

⑦

말하세요.

조용히 하세요.

⑥

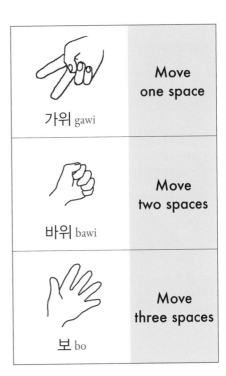

가위 gawi	**Move one space**
바위 bawi	**Move two spaces**
보 bo	**Move three spaces**

1. annyeonghaseyo
2. anjeuseyo ireonaseyo
3. annyeong
4. boseyo deureuseyo
5. seonsaengnim annyeonghaseyo
6. malhaseyo joyonghi haseyo
7. mannaseo bangawoyo
8. chumchuseyo noraehaseyo
9. son deuseyo bal deuseyo
10. annyeong tto mannayo

저는 나미예요.

I am Nami.

Look and Listen 1

TR 08

> 저는
> 나미예요.

> 저는
> 짐(Jim)이에요.

> 저는
> 제니(Jenny)예요.

> 저는
> 송민(Songmin)이에요.

••• Let's Talk

Introduce yourself to five people around you as Nami, Jim, Jenny and Songmin do above.

"저는 **나미**예요."
jeoneun namiyeyo

"저는 **짐**이에요."
jeoneun jimieyo

Let's Move

TR 08

나가세요.
nagaseyo
Please go out.

들어오세요.
deureooseyo
Please come in.

Elementary school students in South Korea study subjects, such as Korean language, social studies, mathematics, science, music, art, physical and moral education. They also study English and continue studying it through middle school and high school. In middle school, students can also choose to study technical and vocational subjects.

In general academic high schools, students study a variety of subjects including Korean language and literature, mathematics, chemistry, physics, biology, English and other foreign languages, history, geography, physical education, music and art. In vocational high schools, agriculture, engineering, business or maritime studies can be studied.

Most elementary school children do not wear uniforms but most middle school and high school students wear uniforms. Boys in middle schools and high schools wear uniforms and must keep their hair short. Girls wear knee-length skirts. Many students like wearing running shoes.

- What subjects do students learn in elementary school in your country?
- What are the different points between your school and Korean schools?

Let's Sing

TR 09

"저는 나미예요."
jeoneun namiyeyo

 안녕하세요?
annyeonghaseyo

안녕하세요?
annyeonghaseyo

만나서 반가워요.
mannaseo bangawoyo

반가워요.
bangawoyo

저는 나미예요.
jeoneun namiyeyo

저는 짐이에요.
jeoneun jimieyo

저는 제니예요.
jeoneun jeniyeyo

저는 송민이에요.
jeoneun songminieyo

안녕하세요?
annyeonghaseyo

안녕하세요?
annyeonghaseyo

만나서 반가워요.
mannaseo bangawoyo

반가워요.
bangawoyo

Make a group of four people. Introduce yourself to your group to the tune of "저는 나미예요."

••• Let's Role-play

저는 학생이에요.
jeoneun haksaengieyo

A group of four peole go outside the classroom when the teacher/class says "나가세요 (nagaseyo)."
They decide who they will be: They can be teachers or pretend to be one of the objects shown below. When the teacher/class says "들어오세요 (deureooseyo)," they come into the classroom and introduce themselves to each other by saying, "안녕하세요? 만나서 반가워요. 저는 _____ 이에/예요."

저는
학생이에요.

 양
yang

 말
mal

 나비
nabi

 별
byeol

 달
dal

Look and Listen 2

TR 09

··· Let's Talk

Ask the names of five people around you just as Nami does above.

"이름이 뭐예요?"

ireumi mwoyeyo

"스노이예요. / 페퍼예요."

seunoiyeyo   pepeoyeyo

 Listen and Check

TR 09

Listen carefully to the following words.

1.	2.	3.	4.	5.
짐	제니	송민	스노이	페퍼
jim	jeni	songmin	seunoi	pepeo

··· Let's Do It Match the picture with the word that is read out.

a. ☐   b. ☐   c. ☐   d. ☐   e. ☐

••• Let's Role-play

이름이 뭐예요?
ireumi mwoyeyo

Imagine that you are a famous star or one of the people whose names are given below. Greet five people using the expressions below.

나미
(Nami)

이안
(Ian)

제니
(Jenny)

짐
(Jim)

미아
(Mia)

송민
(Songmin)

안녕하세요?

저는 **송민**이에요.
이름이 뭐예요?

만나서 반가워요.

안녕! 또 만나요.

안녕하세요?

신데렐라
(Cinderella)예요.

만나서 반가워요.

안녕! 또 만나요.

Let's Learn the Korean Alphabet

 Consonants: ㅅ s   ㅈ j

Letter	Order of Strokes	Practice				
ㅅ	①ㅅ					
ㅈ	②①→ㅈ③					

Vowels: ㅔ e   ㅖ ye

Letter	Order of Strokes	Practice				
ㅔ	②↓ㅔ↓③ ①→					
ㅖ	③↓ ①→ㅖ↓④ ②→					

··· Let's Write

On your partner's hands or back, trace one of the above letters
with your finger, and ask which letter it is.

··· Let's Read

저   짐이에요   제니예요   송민이에요   신데렐라예요

··· Let's Read More

사자   소   아버지   집   모자   레몬

1. Choose the most suitable expression for each of the speech bubbles.

a) 저는 나미예요.	b) 만나서 반가워요.	c) 안녕하세요?
jeoneun namiyeyo	mannaseo bangawoyo	annyeonghaseyo

2. Link the pictures and speech bubbles.

이름이 뭐예요?
ireumi mwoyeyo

1) 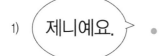 •

• a)

2) 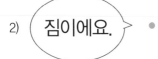 •

• b)

3. Answer the question below by using the names provided in the box.

이안   미아   스노이   신데렐라

이름이 뭐예요?

1)

2)

3)

4)

4. Fill in the blanks with Korean syllables from the box.

서   에   세   예

짐: 안녕하세요?
annyeonghaseyo

제니: 안녕하☐요?
annyeonghaseyo

짐: 저는 짐이☐요.
jeoneun jimieyo

제니: 저는 제니☐요.
jeoneun jeniyeyo

짐: 만나서 반가워요.
mannaseo bangawoyo

제니: 만나☐ 반가워요.
mannaseo bangawoyo

Unit 05

한국 사람이에요?

Are you Korean?

 Look and Listen 1
TR 10

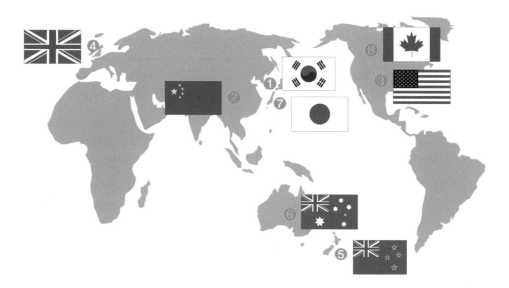

❶ 한국(Korea) ❷ 중국(China) ❸ 미국(USA) ❹ 영국(England)

❺ 뉴질랜드(New Zealand) ❻ 호주(Australia) ❼ 일본(Japan) ❽ 캐나다(Canada)

 Let's Chant
TR 11

Pointing to the countries shown above, repeat after your teacher.

한국	중국	미국	영국
hanguk	jungguk	miguk	yeongguk

뉴질랜드	호주	일본	캐나다
nyujillaendeu	hoju	ilbon	kaenada

따라 하세요.
ttara haseyo

질문하세요.
jilmunhaseyo
Please ask a question.

대답하세요.
daedaphaseyo
Please answer.

Look and Listen 2
TR 11

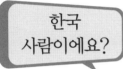

한국
사람이에요?

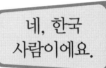

네, 한국
사람이에요.

중국 사람
jungguk saram

미국 사람
miguk saram

영국 사람
yeongguk saram

••• Let's Talk

Pointing to each picture above, ask your partner as Snowy does.

"한국 사람이에요?"
hanguk saramieyo

"네, 한국 사람이에요."
ne hanguk saramieyo

 Additional Words

일본 사람 ilbon saram	호주 사람 hoju saram	캐나다 사람 kaenada saram
뉴질랜드 사람 nyujillaendeu saram	아일랜드(Ireland) 사람 aillaendeu saram	태국(Thailand) 사람 taeguk saram

태극기
taegeukgi

Korean national flag

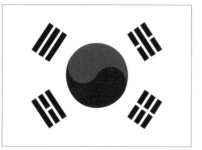

The Korean national flag is called 태극기 (taegeukgi). Its design symbolizes the principles of the universe in Eastern philosophy. It consists of a circle made up of red and blue parts in the center, four sets of black lines in each corner, and a white background. The circle, called *taegeuk*, is made up of two parts which represent the two great forces that run the universe: *yin*, the negative cosmic force, and *yang*, the positive force. *Yang* represents heaven, light and life among other things, while *yin* represents earth, darkness and death. Balance and harmony between these two forces are essential to keep the universe operating in perfect peace, which is symbolized in the shape of a circle. The black lines, broken or whole, represent the four universal elements: heaven (top left); earth (bottom right); fire (bottom left) and water (top right).

- What is the national flag of your country like and what does it symbolize?
- How many countries' national flags do you know?

무궁화
mugunghwa

Rose of Sharon (Korean national flower)

무궁화 (mugunghwa), the Rose of Sharon, is Korea's national flower and has been loved by Koreans for thousands of years. The word *mugunghwa* means "never-ending blossom." The flower looks similar to the hibiscus and blossoms in pink, white, red or purple during summer for about one hundred days, from early July till late October, in most parts of Korea.

- What is the national flower of your country?
- What other national flowers do you know?

··· Let's Talk

Find out where your friends are from by asking questions.

"한국 사람이에요?"
hanguk saramieyo

"아니요, 뉴질랜드 사람이에요."
aniyo nyujilaendeu saramieyo

 Additional Words

인도네시아(Indonesia) indonesia	**말레이시아**(Malaysia) malleisia	**싱가포르**(Singapore) singgaporeu	**인도**(India) indo
필리핀(Philippines) pillipin	**베트남**(Vietnam) beteunam	**브라질**(Brazil) beurajil	**러시아**(Russia) reosia

··· Let's Role-play

한국 사람이에요?
hanguk saramieyo

Imagine that you are a reporter. Interview three people asking questions and thanking them as follows.

실례합니다.
sillyehamnida
Excuse me.

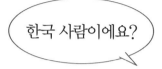
한국 사람이에요?

고맙습니다./
gomapseumnida
감사합니다.*
gamsahamnida

∗ "고맙습니다" and "감사합니다" are the most polite ways of saying "thank you."

Listen and Check

TR 11

Listen carefully to the following words.

1.

한국 사람
hanguk saram

2.

중국 사람
jungguk saram

3.
미국 사람
miguk saram

4.

영국 사람
yeongguk saram

5.

뉴질랜드 사람
nyujillaendeu saram

6.

호주 사람
hoju saram

7.

일본 사람
ilbon saram

8.

캐나다 사람
kaenada saram

··· Let's Do It Match the picture with the word that is read out.

a. ☐   b. ☐   c. ☐   d. ☐

e. ☐   f. ☐   g. ☐   h. ☐

Let's Learn the Korean Alphabet

🔊 Consonant: ㄱ g/k

Letter	Order of Strokes	Practice				
ㄱ	ㄱ↓					

When "ㄱ" comes at the final position of a syllable and a vowel does not follow it, it is usually pronounced [k].

🔊 Vowels: ㅜ u   ㅠ yu

Letter	Order of Strokes	Practice				
ㅜ	①→ ㅜ ↓②					
ㅠ	②↓ ①→ ㅠ ↓③					

••• Let's Write

On your partner's hands or back, trace one of the above letters with your finger, and ask which letter it is.

••• Let's Read

한국   중국   미국   영국   뉴질랜드

••• Let's Read More

아기   가방   고양이   공   주스   우유

Let's Review

1. Answer Snowy's question.

한국
사람이에요?

2. Complete the crossword.

Across: Korea

Down: U.S.A.

미

한

3. Check the right box.

	한국 사람	미국 사람	뉴질랜드 사람	호주 사람
1) 세종대왕 (King Sejong the Great)	V			
2) 에드먼드 힐러리 (Edmund Hillary)				
3) 니콜 키드먼 (Nicole Kidman)				
4) 마이클 조던 (Michael Jordan)				

4. Draw a line to match the correct response to the question.

1) 한국 사람이에요?
   hanguk saramieyo

2) 호주 사람이에요?
   hoju saramieyo

3) 미국 사람이에요?
   miguk saramieyo

a) 네, 한국 사람이에요.
   ne hanguk saramieyo

b) 아니요, 뉴질랜드 사람이에요.
   aniyo nyujillaendeu saramieyo

c) 네, 호주 사람이에요.
   ne hoju saramieyo

어디에 살아요?
Where do you live?

Look and Listen 1

TR 12

뉴질랜드	미국	중국	호주
nyujillaendeu	miguk	jungguk	hoju

••• Let's Talk

Pointing to the countries on the map above, ask your partner where they live.

"어디에 살아요?"   "한국에 살아요."
eodie sarayo   hanguge sarayo

호랑이, 진돗개, 삽살개

horangi   jindotgae   sapsalgae

Siberian tigers used to roam freely from the northern most highlands to the southern most provinces of Korea. Villagers in mountainous areas were very afraid of them. However, tigers have not been captured in South Korea since 1922. Tigers most probably still live around Mt. Baekdusan, the highest mountain on the Korean Peninsula. Tigers, called 호랑이 (horangi), often appear as the main character in Korean folk tales and folk paintings. The mascot for the 1988 Seoul Olympic Games was a baby tiger named 호돌이 (hodori).

Korea has two unique species of dog called 진돗개 (jindotgae) and 삽살개 (sapsalgae). Originally from Jindo Island, to the south of the Korean Peninsula, *jindotgae* are renowned for their intelligence and bravery. The long-haired *sapsalgae* is also much loved by Koreans. Dogs are people's most favorite pet in Korea.

- What animal do people love most in your country?
- What animal is popular in folk/fairy tales in your home country?

Look and Listen 2

••• Let's Talk

Pointing to the people above, ask your partner where they live.

"어디에 살아요?"
eodie sarayo

"서울에 살아요."
seoure sarayo

••• **Let's Talk**

Ask a question to five people around you and find out where they live.

"**어디에 살아요?**"   "**알바니에 살아요.**"

eodie sarayo   albanie sarayo

노스코트   노스크로스   켈스톤
noseukoteu   noseukeuroseu   kelseuton
                                                                        _____

TR 12

Let's Move

앞으로 가세요.
apeuro gaseyo

Please go forward.

뒤로 가세요.
dwiro gaseyo

Please go backward.

Let's Sing

 타잔 씨, 타잔 씨, 어디에 살아요?
tajan ssi tajan ssi eodie sarayo

정글에 살아요. 정글에 살아요.
jeonggeure sarayo   jeonggeure sarayo

* The word "씨(ssi)" is added to one's first name to show respect.

Let's Sing with Actions

Divide the class into two groups, A and B. Adding "씨(ssi)" to the name of a group B member, the group A marches forward asking where he/she lives to the tune of the first line. The person whose name has been called says where he/she lives to the tune of the second line.

··· Let's Role-play

어디에 살아요?
eodie sarayo

Imagine that you are a reporter. Interview three people asking questions and thank them as follows.

실례합니다. 이름이 뭐예요?

어디에 살아요?

고맙습니다. / 감사합니다.

해리(Harry)예요.

* Remember, the interviewer should be polite.

TR 13

Listen and Check

Listen carefully to the following words.

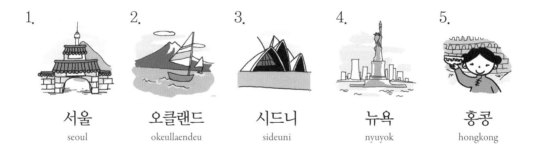

1.	2.	3.	4.	5.
서울	오클랜드	시드니	뉴욕	홍콩
seoul	okeullaendeu	sideuni	nyuyok	hongkong

··· **Let's Do It** Match the picture with the word that is read out.

a. ☐　　b. ☐　　c. ☐　　d. ☐　　e. ☐

Let's Learn the Korean Alphabet

Consonants: ㅋ k ㅎ h

Letter	Order of Strokes	Practice				
ㅋ	①→ ㅋ ②→					
ㅎ	②→①→ ㅎ ③					

Vowel: ㅐ ae

Letter	Order of Strokes	Practice				
ㅐ	①↓ ㅐ ②→ ③↓					

••• Let's Write

On your partner's hands or back, trace one of the above letters with your finger, and ask which letter it is.

••• Let's Read

캐나다   한국   호주   홍콩   뉴질랜드   오클랜드

••• Let's Read More

카메라   학교   개   개미   캥거루   해

1. Answer Snowy's question.

어디에 살아요?

2. Answer the questions using the words provided in the box.

중국	미국	뉴질랜드	호주
jungguk	miguk	nyujillaendeu	hoju

어디에 살아요?
eodie sarayo

1)

_____

2)

_____

3)

_____

4)

_____

3. Snowy is interviewing Hodori and Harry. Fill in the blanks with Korean syllables from the box.

이름	해리	에	예	한

1) 스노이: 이름이 뭐예요?
ireumi mwoyeyo

호돌이: 호돌이예요.
hodoriyeyo

스노이: 어디☐ 살아요?
eodie sarayo

호돌이: ☐국에 살아요.
hanguge sarayo

2) 스노이: ☐☐이 뭐예요?
ireumi mwoyeyo

해 리: 저는 해리☐요.
jeoneun haeriyeyo

스노이: ☐☐씨, 어디에 살아요?
haerissi, eodie sarayo

해 리: 영국☐ 살아요.
yeongguge sarayo

Let's Play a Game   "실레합니다."   Excuse me.
sillyehamnida

■ **Aim:** To complete an interview

■ **Method:** Groups of two or three students get together with a marker/playing piece for each player. A game of "Rock, paper and scissors" is played by saying "gawi, bawi, bo" to decide who starts the game for each round. The winner starts the conversation in space 1 and the others reply with the appropriate answer. At each round, "gawi, bawi, bo" is played and the winner moves the number of spaces as in the table on page 31. Players who make a mistake go back one space. Those who land on space 2 or 7 must finish the task and then go to space 4, where a task needs to be performed.

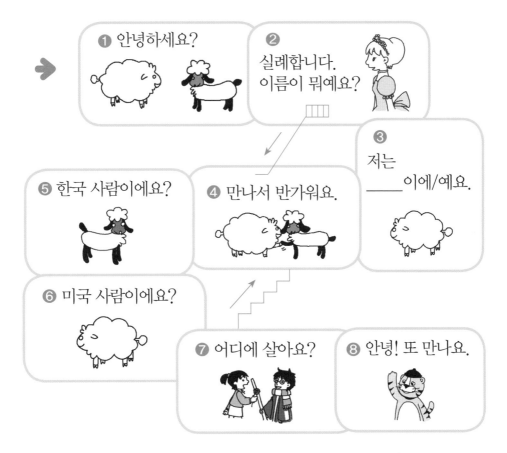

1. annyeonghaseyo
2. sillyehamnida
   ireumi mwoyeyo
3. jeoneun ___ ie / yeyo
4. mannaseo bangawoyo
5. hanguk saramieyo
6. miguk saramieyo
7. eodie sarayo
8. annyeong tto mannayo

피터 어디 있어요?

Where is Peter?

Look and Listen 1

TR 14

나미 있어요?

짐 있어요?

한국어

네, 있어요.

아니요, 없어요.

••• Let's Talk

Answer the roll call.

"**나미 있어요?**"
nami isseoyo

"**네, 있어요./아니요, 없어요.**"
ne isseoyo   aniyo eopseoyo

Let's Move

TR 14

여기 보세요.
yeogi boseyo
Please look here.

저기 보세요.
jeogi boseyo
Please look there.

Look and Listen 2

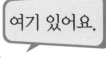

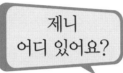

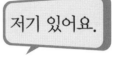

··· Let's Talk

Using the names of five people around you, ask where they are.

"피터 어디 있어요?"
piteo eodi isseoyo

"여기 있어요."
yeogi isseoyo

"제니 어디 있어요?"
jeni eodi isseoyo

"저기 있어요."
jeogi isseoyo

TR 15

Let's Sing   "피터팬(Peter Pan), 어디 있어요?"
piteopaen eodi isseoyo

    피터팬, 피터팬, 어디 있어요?
piteopaen piteopaen eodi isseoyo

여기 있어요. 여기 있어요. 안녕하세요.

yeogi isseoyo   yeogi isseoyo   annyeonghaseyo

Let's Sing
with Actions

After some of the students hide, the rest of the class starts
singing the song. The person whose name has been called
comes out and sings the second line.

Look and Listen 3

페퍼, 화장실
pepeo hwajangsil

이안, 수영장
ian suyeongjang

아나, 테니스장
ana   teniseujang

⋯ Let's Talk

Pointing at each picture above ask where the people or animals are.

"스노이 어디 있어요?"
seunoi eodi isseoyo

"교실에 있어요."
gyosire isseoyo

Additional Words

도서관	doseogwan	library	강당	gangdang	assembly hall
운동장	undongjang	playing field/stadium	집	jip	house/home

Traditional Korean houses are called 한옥 (hanok). The frame of these houses is built with wood, the walls of clay and stone, and the roof is made with tiles or rice stalks. *Hanok* have a spacious wooden floor hall in the center and floor-heated rooms. The wooden floor of the hall provides cool air circulation in summer and the heated floor, 온돌 (ondol), quickly warms the rooms in winter.

From the late 20th century, apartments have become popular. Today, about half of the population of South Korea lives in apartments. Modern apartments are often equipped with the floor-heating system and air conditioners.

- What are the devices for heating and cooling houses in your country?
- What does a traditional house look like in your country?

··· Let's Role-play

어디 있어요?
eodi isseoyo

Let each member of your group choose to act as one of the characters shown below. In turn, ask them where they are and guess what their names are as follows.

어디 있어요?
eodi isseoyo

교실에 있어요.
gyosire isseoyo

페퍼예요?
pepeoyeyo

아니요.
aniyo

스노이예요?
seunoiyeyo

네, 스노이예요.
ne seunoiyeyo

1)

2)

3)

Listen carefully to the following words.

1.

피터
piteo

2.

교실
gyosil

3.

화장실
hwajangsil

4.

수영장
suyeongjang

5.

테니스장
teniseujang

··· **Let's Do It** Match the picture with the word that is read out.

a. ☐

b. ☐

c. ☐

d. ☐

e. ☐

Consonants: ㅌ t ㅍ p

Letter	Order of Strokes	Practice				
ㅌ	ㅌ					
ㅍ	ㅍ					

Vowel: ㅘ wa = ㅗ + ㅏ

Letter	Order of Strokes	Practice				
ㅘ	ㅘ					

··· Let's Write

On your partner's hands or back, trace one of the above letters with your finger, and ask which letter it is.

··· Let's Read

피터   팬   페퍼   테니스장   화장실

··· Let's Read More

토마토   텔레비전   택시   피아노   사과   전화기

1. Mark who is present and who is absent in the class.

	있어요	없어요
1) 미아 (Mia)	V	
2) 짐 (Jim)		
3) 피터 (Peter)		
4) 제니 (Jenny)		
5) 이안 (Ian)		
6) 나미 (Nami)		

2. Complete the crossword.

Across: Here

Down: There

	저
여	

3. Fill in the blanks with Korean syllables from the box.

피터	여기	에	화

선생님: ☐☐ 있어요?
piteo isseoyo

피 터: 네, 있어요.
ne isseoyo

선생님: 어디 있어요?
eodi isseoyo

피 터: ☐☐ 있어요.
yeogi isseoyo

선생님: 짐 어디 있어요?
jim eodi isseoyo

피 터: ☐장실☐ 있어요.
hwajangsire isseoyo

이게 뭐예요?
What is this?

 Look and Listen 1
TR 16

칠판
chilpan

컴퓨터
keompyuteo

시계
sigye

··· Let's Talk

Pointing to the objects above, ask your partner what each one is. Take turns with your partner.

"이게 뭐예요?"   "의자예요. / 책상이에요."
ige mwoyeyo   uijayeyo   chaeksangieyo

The traditional Korean costume is called 한복 (hanbok). In the past, people who were rich wore *hanbok* made of silk that were very elegant and luxurious, while ordinary people wore *hanbok* made of cotton that were simple in design and color. In modern Korea, the *hanbok* is often worn on festival days or on special occasions, such as special birthdays or weddings. Recently, Korean fashion designers have modified the design of the traditional *hanbok* into a more practical outfit, encouraging people to wear it in everyday life.

- Have you ever seen a *hanbok* in person?
- Have you ever worn a *hanbok*?
- What are the different parts that make up a *hanbok*?

조끼
jokki

저고리
jeogori

저고리
jeogori

바지
baji

치마
chima

버선
beoseon

고무신
gomusin

문
mun

창문
changmun

시계
sigye

··· Let's Talk

Pointing to an object which is far away from you, ask your partner what it is.
Take turns with your partner.

"저게 뭐예요?"
jeoge mwoyeyo

"지도예요. / 문이에요."
jidoyeyo   munieyo

Let's Move

책 펴세요.
chaek pyeoseyo

Please open the book.

책 덮으세요.
chaek deopeuseyo

Please close the book.

Look and Listen 3

••• Let's Talk

Work with your partner. Pointing at an object in the classroom, one of you asks what it is. The other answers and asks whether the answer is right.

"이게 뭐예요?"　　"의자예요. 맞아요?"　　"맞아요./틀려요."
ige mwoyeyo　　uijayeyo　　majayo　　majayo　　teullyeoyo

That's right. / That's wrong.

Let's Sing   "이게 뭐예요?"
ige mwoyeyo

 이게 뭐예요?
ige mwoyeyo

컴퓨터예요.
keompyuteoyeyo

저게 뭐예요?
jeoge mwoyeyo

창문이에요.
changmunieyo

Let's Sing with Actions   Pointing at things close by and then far away, a student asks the questions, "이게 뭐예요?" "저게 뭐예요?" to the above tune. The rest of the class answers to the same tune.

이게
뭐예요?

바지예요.

 ## Listen and Check

Listen carefully to the following words.

1.
2.
3.
4.
5.

의자	책상	칠판	창문	컴퓨터
uija	chaeksang	chilpan	changmun	keompyuteo

••• **Let's Do It**   Match the picture with the word that is read out.

a. ☐   b. ☐   c. ☐   d. ☐   e. ☐

68 | Time for Korean 1

Let's Learn the Korean Alphabet

 **Consonant:** ㅊ ch

Letter	Order of Strokes	Practice				
ㅊ	ㅊ					

 **Vowels:** ㅝ wo = ㅜ + ㅓ   ㅢ ui = ㅡ + ㅣ

Letter	Order of Strokes	Practice				
ㅝ	ㅝ					
ㅢ	ㅢ					

••• Let's Write

On your partner's hands or back, trace one of the above letters with your finger, and ask which letter it is.

••• Let's Read

책상   칠판   창문   뭐   의자

••• Let's Read More

차   치마   치약   치즈   의사

1. Choose the right answer to the question.

1) 이게 뭐예요? (   )
   ige mwoyeyo

   a) 의자예요.
   b) 책상이에요.

2) 저게 뭐예요? (   )
   jeoge mwoyeyo

   a) 시계예요.
   b) 칠판이에요.

2. Complete the crossword.

   Across: Doctor

   Down: Chair

3. Answer the question using the words provided in the box.

치즈	차	치약	시계	치마
chijeu	cha	chiyak	sigye	chima

이게
뭐예요?

1)

_____

2)
_____

3)

_____

4)
_____

5)

_____

4. Fill in the blanks with Korean syllables from the box.

| 뭐 | 의자 | 창 | 문 | 책 |

1) 나 미: 이게 뭐예요?
ige mwoyeyo

페 퍼: ☐이에요.
munieyo

2) 나 미: 저게 ☐예요?
jeoge mwoyeyo

페 퍼: ☐☐예요.
uijayeyo

3) 나 미: 이게 뭐예요?
ige mwoyeyo

스노이: ☐상이에요. 맞아요?
chaeksangieyo   majayo

나 미: 맞아요.
majayo

4) 나 미: 이게 ☐예요?
ige mwoyeyo

스노이: 칠판이에요. 맞아요?
chilpanieyo   majayo

나 미: 틀려요. ☐문이에요.
teullyeoyo   changmunieyo

지우개 있어요?

Do you have an eraser?

Look and Listen 1

TR 18

책	공책	연필	필통	자
chaek	gongchaek	yeonpil	piltong	ja

••• Let's Talk

Ask five people around you what they have. Use the items given above.

"**지우개** 있어요?"
jiugae isseoyo

"네, **지우개** 있어요."
ne jiugae isseoyo

"**종이** 있어요?"
jongi isseoyo

"아니요, **종이** 없어요."
aniyo jongi eopseoyo

TR 19

Let's Sing "지우개 있어요?"
jiugae isseoyo

 지우개 있어요? 지우개 있어요?
jiugae isseoyo   jiugae isseoyo

네, 있어요. 지우개 있어요.
ne isseoyo   jiugae isseoyo

종이 있어요? 종이 있어요?
jongi isseoyo   jongi isseoyo

아니요, 없어요. 종이 없어요.
aniyo eopseoyo   jongi eopseoyo

 **Let's Sing with Actions**

Divide the class into four groups. Each group has four stationery items. Holding one of the items, each group in turn asks whether the other groups have it to the tune of the first line. The other groups answer to the tune of the second line.

 Let's Chant

TR 19

As your teacher reads each stationery item, repeat after him/her and point to the correct word.

책	공책	연필	필통
chaek	gongchaek	yeonpil	piltong

자	종이	지우개
ja	jongi	jiugae

따라 읽으세요.
ttara ilgeuseyo

 Let's Move

TR 19

따라 읽으세요.
ttara ilgeuseyo
Please read after me.

쓰세요.
sseuseyo
Please write.

호랑이와 곶감

The tiger and the dried persimmon

horangiwa gotgam

Once upon a time, deep in the mountain, there lived a mother and baby with their cow. There also lived a great big tiger who roamed around and caught whatever he wanted to eat. Everyone in the mountain was afraid of the tiger.

One dark night, the tiger went to find something to eat. He smelt the cow and went to the house where the cow was. The tiger was about to jump into the shed where the cow was sleeping, but suddenly he heard a noise. The baby was crying loudly in the house!

The tiger wondered what was going on. He crept up to the house and heard the baby's mother soothing the baby, "Darling, stop crying and go to sleep." But the baby kept crying. Then the mother said "Darling, stop crying. A great big tiger is at the door!" But the baby only cried louder! The tiger almost fainted when he heard this. 'How does she know I'm at the door?' He wondered.

Then the mother said, "Darling, stop crying. Here's a dried persimmon, 곶감 (gotgam)." Immediately the baby stopped crying. The tiger was stunned at the sudden silence. He had never seen a dried persimmon. He muttered "I thought that I was the strongest in the mountain, but *gotgam* must be even stronger than me! Even the mention of *gotgam* stopped the baby crying!" Frightened, the tiger slowly walked away from the house towards the shed.

At the same time a thief approached the shed to steal the cow. Seeing an animal in the dark moving near the shed, he mistook the tiger for the cow! The thief pounced on the back of the tiger. Shocked at the sudden attack and thinking *gotgam* had landed on his back, the tiger started running.

The thief too was shocked by the tiger suddenly running. He held the tiger's back tightly so he wouldn't fall off. The tiger ran and ran with the thief on his back. He ran the whole night until sunrise.

At dawn, the thief saw he had been riding a tiger, not a cow! When the tired tiger passed under a low tree branch, he quickly grabbed the branch, jumped off the tiger and hid among trees.

The tiger thought that the terribly strong 곶감 (gotgam) had finally gotten off his back. Much relieved, he felt he was safe at last. The tiger never attempted to visit the house where the baby and the mother lived again.

- Why do you think the baby stopped crying when it saw a dried persimmon?
- Have you tasted fresh persimmons?
- Have you tasted dried persimmons? Would you like to see or taste dried persimmons?
- Which dried fruits have you tasted?
- Which dried fruits do you like?

Look and Listen 2

질문 있어요?

연필깎이예요.

네, 있어요.
이게 뭐예요?

••• **Let's Talk**

Ask your partner whether he/she has a question. Your partner will point to
one of the pictures below and ask you what it is.

"질문 있어요?"
jilmun isseoyo
Do you have a question?

"네, 있어요. 이게 뭐예요?"
ne isseoyo   ige mwoyeyo

"연필깎이예요."
yeonpilkkakiyeyo

책
chaek

공책
gongchaek

연필깎이
yeonpilkkaki

연필
yeonpil

필통
piltong

자
ja

Listen and Check

Listen carefully to the following words.

1.
책
chaek

2.
연필
yeonpil

3.
필통
piltong

4.
연필깎이
yeonpilkkaki

5.
자
ja

••• **Let's Do It** Match the picture with the word that is read out.

a. ☐   b. ☐   c. ☐   d. ☐   e. ☐

Let's Learn the Korean Alphabet

TR 19

🔊 Consonants:　　ㄲ kk　　ㄸ tt　　ㅃ pp　　ㅆ ss

Letter	Order of Strokes	Practice				
ㄲ	ㄲ					
ㄸ	ㄸ					
ㅃ	ㅃ					
ㅆ	ㅆ					

••• Let's Write

On your partner's hands or back, trace one of the above letters with your finger, and ask which letter it is.

••• Let's Read

연필깎이　　　도깨비　　　뚝딱　　　있어요　　　쓰세요

••• Let's Read More

꼬리　　　　코끼리　　　땅콩　　　　빵　　　쓰레기통

Let's Review

1. Answer Snowy's question.

2. Complete the crossword.

   Across: Pencil

   Down: Pencilcase

3. Fill in the blanks with Korean syllables from the box.

> 지우개   자   있어   깎이

1) 송민: 지우개 있어요?
    jiugae isseoyo

   미야: 네, ☐☐☐ 있어요.
    ne jiugae isseoyo

2) 송민: 자 있어요?
    ja isseoyo

   미야: 아니요, ☐ 없어요.
    aniyo ja eopseoyo

3) 아냐: 질문 있어요?
    jilmun isseoyo

   페퍼: 네, ☐☐요. 이게 뭐예요?
    ne isseoyo   ige mwoyeyo

   아냐: 연필☐☐예요.
    yeonpilkkakiyeyo

Let's Play a Game   "나미 있어요?"   Is Nami in?
nami isseoyo

❶ 나미 있어요?

❷ 짐 있어요?

❻ 저게 뭐예요?

시작

❺ 이게 뭐예요?

❸ 스노이 어디 있어요?

❹ 아나 어디 있어요?

■ **Aim**: To play a game called "School"

■ **Method**: Groups of two or three students get together with a counter/playing piece for each player. A game of "Rock, paper and scissors" is played by saying "gawi, bawi, bo" to decide who starts the game for each round. The winner starts the conversation in space 1 and the others reply with appropriate actions. At each round, "gawi, bawi, bo" is played and the winner moves the number of spaces as in the table on page 31. The person who gets to the end first is the winner. Players can create new games by changing the names or objects on the board.

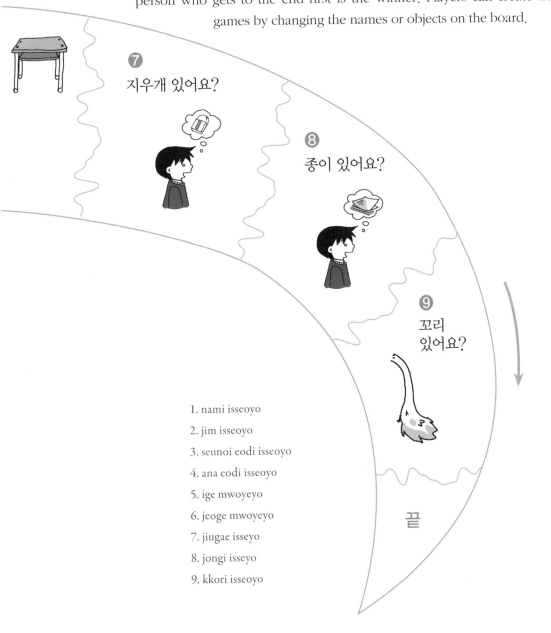

❼ 지우개 있어요?

❽ 종이 있어요?

❾ 꼬리 있어요?

1. nami isseoyo

2. jim isseoyo

3. seunoi eodi isseoyo

4. ana eodi isseoyo

5. ige mwoyeyo

6. jeoge mwoyeyo

7. jiugae isseyo

8. jongi isseyo

9. kkori isseoyo

끝

Unit 10

펜 좀 주세요.
Please give me a pen.

🎧 Look and Listen 1
TR 20

풀	색종이	크레용	휴지
pul	saekjongi	keureyong	hyuji

••• Let's Talk

Ask five people around you for something and thank them when they give it to you.

"펜 좀 주세요."
pen jom juseyo

"여기 있어요."
yeogi isseoyo

"고맙습니다."
gomapseumnida

"천만에요."
cheonmaneyo
You're welcome.

Look and Listen 2

••• Let's Talk

Ask three people around you for something, and tell them it is alright when they say they're sorry because they don't have it/them.

"**가위** 좀 주세요."
gawi jom juseyo

"없어요. 미안해요."
eopseoyo   mianhaeyo

"괜찮아요."
gwaenchanayo

요요
yoyo

카메라
kamera

땅콩
ttangkong

빵
ppang

 TR 20   Let's Move

시작하세요.   Start
sijakhaseyo
Please start.

그만하세요.   Stop
geumanhaseyo
Please stop.

탈춤 　Mask dance
talchum

There are many types of Korean dances, but the mask dance is the most fun with its humorous stories and funny masks. In the Lion Dance, the lion, danced by two people under one costume, disciplines bad people by threatening to eat them. Another mask dance makes fun of a thick-headed nobleman and a corrupt monk. Most characters, including the bride, are played by men.

　Mask dances have traditionally been performed in villages in the country during festivals such as Chuseok (Korean Thanksgiving). Today, they are also performed on stage.

• Which mask do you think is worn for each character in the mask dance?
　Link the mask and the character below.

1. 양반
yangban

2. 먹중
meokjung

3. 각시
gaksi

a. the corrupt monk　　　b. the bride　　　c. the foolish

Listen and Check

Listen carefully to the following words.

1.

펜
pen

2.

풀
pul

3.

색종이
saekjongi

4.

크레용
keureyong

5.

휴지
hyuji

••• **Let's Do It** Match the picture with the word that is read out.

a.   b.   c.   d.   e. ☐

Let's Sing "오리는 꽥꽥"
orineun kkwaek-kkwaek

오리는 꽥꽥
orineun kkwaek-kkwaek

새는 짹짹
saeneun jjaek-jjaek

돼지는 꿀꿀
dwaejineun kkul-kkul

나는 깔깔
naneun kkal-kkal

오리는 꽥꽥
orineun kkwaek-kkwaek

새는 짹짹
saeneun jjaek-jjaek

돼지는 꿀꿀
dwaejineun kkul-kkul

나는 깔깔
naneun kkal-kkal

Let's Sing with Actions

Everybody imitates the movement of each animal as it comes up in the song.

꽥꽥

짹짹

꿀꿀

••• Let's Role-play

새예요!
saeyeyo

Imagine that you are one of the animals below. After making its sound, the others try and guess what you are by saying, for example, "새예요! (saeyeyo You are a bird!)" If their guess is correct, say "맞아요(majayo)," and if their guess is wrong, say "틀려요(teullyeoyo)."

Others	Student 1
	"꿀꿀!" kkul-kkul
오리예요! oriyeyo	틀려요. teullyeoyo
돼지예요! dwaejiyeyo	맞아요. majayo

Optional Addition

Others	Student 2
이름이 뭐예요? ireumi mwoyeyo	_____
어디에 살아요? eodie sarayo	_____
이게 뭐예요? ige mwoyeyo	_____

Let's Learn the Korean Alphabet

Consonant: ㅉ jj

Letter	Order of Strokes	Practice				
ㅉ	①→②→④⑤③→⑥					

Vowels: ㅙ wae = ㅗ + ㅐ   ㅟ wi = ㅜ + ㅣ

Letter	Order of Strokes	Practice				
ㅙ						
ㅟ						

••• Let's Write

On your partner's hands or back, trace one of the above letters with your finger, and ask which letter it is.

••• Let's Read

괜찮아요   가위   바위

••• Let's Read More

짹짹   돼지   꽥꽥   키위   펭귄

1. Draw a line to connect the statement to the corresponding reply.

1) 펜 좀 주세요. ●
pen jom juseyo

● a) 천만에요.
cheonmaneyo

2) 고맙습니다. ●
gomapseumnida

● b) 여기 있어요.
yeogi isseoyo

2. Fill in the blanks with Korean syllables from the box.

위   좀   괜

1) 제니: 풀 ☐ 주세요.
pul jom juseyo

잠: 여기 있어요.
yeogi isseoyo

제니: 고맙습니다.
gomapseumnida

잠: 천만에요.
cheonmaneyo

2) 제니: 가☐ 좀 주세요.
gawi jom juseyo

잠: 없어요. 미안해요.
eopseoyo mianhaeyo

제니: ☐찮아요.
gwaenchanayo

3. Draw a line to connect the corresponding sound to each animal.

1) 오리는 ●

2) 돼지는 ●

3) 새는 ●

4) 나는 ●

● a) 짹짹

● b) 꿀꿀

● c) 꽥꽥

● d) 깔깔

APPENDIX

Checklist

Unit 01

After the lesson, check whether you can:

- [ ] greet people in Korean.
- [ ] ask people to stand up and to sit down.
- [ ] read and write words with ㅇ [ ]/ng, ㄴ n, ㅣ i, ㅏ a and ㅑ ya.

Unit 02

After the lesson, check whether you can:

- [ ] tell people that you are glad to meet them.
- [ ] say good-bye.
- [ ] ask people to sing and to dance.
- [ ] read and write words with ㅁ m, ㅂ b, ㅓ eo and ㅕ yeo.

Unit 03

After the lesson, check whether you can:

- [ ] ask people to look and listen.
- [ ] ask people to speak and then to be quiet.
- [ ] ask people to raise a hand and then put it down.
- [ ] ask people to repeat after you.
- [ ] read and write words with ㄷ d, ㄹ r/l, ㅡ eo, ㅗ o and ㅛ yo.

Unit 04

After the lesson, check whether you can:

- [ ] introduce yourself to others.
- [ ] ask people what their names are.
- [ ] ask people to go out and to come in.
- [ ] remember the words for certain animals, fruit and other items that you have learned.
- [ ] read and write words with ㅅ s, ㅈ j, ㅔ e and ㅖ ye.

Unit 05

After the lesson, check whether you can:

- [ ] ask people about their nationality.
- [ ] use 네(ne) and 아니요(aniyo) properly.
- [ ] thank others.
- [ ] invite others to ask questions and to reply.
- [ ] read and write words with ㄱ g/k, ㅜ u and ㅠ yu.

Unit 06

After the lesson, check whether you can:

- ☐ ask people where they live.
- ☐ remember the names of the countries that you have learned.
- ☐ remember the names of the cities that you have learned.
- ☐ ask your friends to go forward and then backward.
- ☐ read words with ㅋ k, ㅎ h and ㅐ ae.

Unit 07

After the lesson, check whether you can:

- ☐ ask if someone is present.
- ☐ ask where others are.
- ☐ remember the names of places that you have learned.
- ☐ ask people to look here and there.
- ☐ read words with ㅌ t, ㅍ p and ㅘ wa.

Unit 08

After the lesson, check whether you can:

- ☐ ask people what things are near you and what things are far away from you.
- ☐ remember the names of things that you have learned so far.
- ☐ ask people to open a book and to close it.
- ☐ read words with ㅊ ch, ㅝ wo and ㅢ ui.

Unit 09

After the lesson, check whether you can:

- ☐ ask people whether they have certain stationery items.
- ☐ ask people whether they have any questions.
- ☐ remember the names of some stationery items.
- ☐ ask people to read after you and to write.
- ☐ read words with ㄲ kk, ㄸ tt, ㅃ pp and ㅆ ss.

Unit 10

After the lesson, check whether you can:

- ☐ ask your friend to give/lend you a stationery item.
- ☐ tell your friend that you are sorry.
- ☐ ask people to start and then to stop doing something.
- ☐ read words with ㅉ jj, ㅙ wae and ㅟ wi.
- ☐ make animal sounds in Korean.

Answers

Unit 01

Listen and Check p.13

a. 3 b. 1 c. 2 d. 5 e. 4

한글 (The Korean alphabet) p.14

ㅛ: yo ㅠ: yu

Let's Review p.17

1. 안녕하세요 2. 1) b 2) a

3. 안 4. 이, 나, 안

Unit 02

Listen and Check p.20

a. 2 b. 1 c. 3 d. 4

Let's Review p.23

1. 반가워요 2. 1) a 2) b

3. 나 4. 1) 반 2) 안녕, 만나

Unit 03

Listen and Check p.26

a. 3 b. 2 c. 5 d. 1 e. 4

Let's Review p.29

1. 1) e 2) c 3) a 4) d 5) f 6) b

2. 요, 요

3. 1) 보 2) 들으 3) 요 4) 손, 요

Unit 04

Listen and Check p.35

a. 3 b. 4 c. 2 d. 1 e. 5

Let's Review p.38

1. 1) c 2) a 3) b

2. 1) b 2) a

3. 1) 미아예요. 2) 스노이예요.

   3) 이안이에요. 4) 신데렐라예요.

4. 세, 에, 예, 서

Unit 05

Listen and Check p.44

a. 1 b. 3 c. 2 d. 4

e. 5 f. 8 g. 6 h. 7

Let's Review p.46

2. 국

3. 1) 한국 사람

   2) 뉴질랜드 사람

   3) 호주 사람

   4) 미국 사람

4. 1) a 2) c 3) b

Unit 06

Listen and Check p.52

a. 1 b. 3 c. 2 d. 4 e. 5

Let's Review p.54

2. 1) 중국에 살아요.   2) 호주에 살아요.
   3) 뉴질랜드에 살아요. 4) 미국에 살아요.
3. 1) 에, 한 2) 이름, 예, 해리, 에

Unit 07

Listen and Check p.61

a. 2 b. 5 c. 4 d. 3 e. 1

Let's Review p.63

1. 1) 있어요   2) 없어요
   3) 있어요   4) 있어요
   5) 없어요   6) 없어요
2. 기
3. 피터, 여기, 화, 에

Unit 08

Listen and Check p.68

a. 5 b. 1 c. 2 d. 4 e. 3

Let's Review p.70

1. 1) a   2) b
2. 의
3. 1) 차예요.   2) 치즈예요. 3)시계예요.
   4) 치마예요. 5) 치약이에요.
4. 1) 문 2) 뭐, 의자 3) 책 4) 뭐, 창

Unit 09

Listen and Check p.75

a. 5 b. 1 c. 2 d. 3 e. 4

Let's Review p.77

2. 필
3. 1) 지우개 2) 자 3) 있어, 깎이

Unit 10

한국 탈 (Korean masks) p.82

1. c 2. a 3. b

Listen and Check p.83

a. 2 b. 1 c. 5 d. 3 e. 4

Let's Review p.86

1. 1) b   2) a
2. 1) 좀 2) 위, 괜
3. 1) c   2) b   3) a   4) d

List of Words and Phrases

Unit 01 안녕하세요?

안녕하세요?	annyeonghaseyo	Hello!/Hi!
선생님	seonsaengnim	teacher
아나	ana	Ana
이안	ian	Ian
안녕?	annyeong	Hi!/Hey!
한국어	hangugeo	Korean language
한글	hangeul	Korean alphabet (written)
세종대왕	sejongdaewang	King Sejong the Great
아이	ai	child
양	yang	sheep
일어나세요.	ireonaseyo	Please stand up.
앉으세요.	anjeuseyo	Please sit down.

Unit 02 만나서 반가워요.

만나서 반가워요.	mannaseo bangawoyo	Glad to meet you.
나미	nami	Nami
어니	eoni	Ernie
안녕!	anneyong	Good-bye!
또	tto	again
만나요.	mannayo	Let's meet.
한국	hanguk	Korea
어머니	eomeoni	mother
바나나	banana	banana
나비	nabi	butterfly
노래하세요.	noraehaseyo	Please sing.
춤추세요.	chumchuseyo	Please dance.

Unit 03 보세요.

보세요.	boseyo	Please look.
들으세요.	deureuseyo	Please listen.
말하세요.	malhaseyo	Please talk.
조용히 하세요.	joyonghi haseyo	Please be quiet.
손 드세요.	son deuseyo	Please raise your hand.
손 내리세요.	son naeriseyo	Please lower your hand.
학교	hakgyo	school
달	dal	moon
돈	don	money
말	mal	horse
별	byeol	star
라디오	radio	radio
요요	yoyo	yoyo
따라 하세요.	ttara haseyo	Please do as I do.
발 드세요.	bal deuseyo	Please lift up your foot.
가위	gawi	scissors
바위	bawi	rock
보	bo	handkerchief/paper

Unit 04 저는 나미예요.

저	jeo	I (humble)
‑는	neun	topic marker
‑예요/‑이에요	yeyo / ieyo	am/are/is
이름	ireum	name
뭐	mwo	what
짐	jim	Jim
제니	jeni	Jenny
송민	songmin	Songmin (Korean name)
학생	haksaeng	student
스노이	seunoi	Snowy
페퍼	pepeo	Pepper
미아	mia	Mia
신데렐라	sinderella	Cinderella
사자	saja	lion
소	so	cow/ox
아버지	abeoji	father
집	jip	house
모자	moja	hat/cap
레몬	remon	lemon
나가세요.	nagaseyo	Please go out.
들어오세요.	deureooseyo	Please come in.

Unit 05 한국 사람이에요?

한국	hanguk	Korea
사람	saram	person
네	ne	yes
아니요	aniyo	no
중국	jungguk	China
미국	miguk	U.S.A.
영국	yeongguk	England
뉴질랜드	nyujillaendeu	New Zealand
호주	hoju	Australia
일본	ilbon	Japan
캐나다	kaenada	Canada
아일랜드	aillaendeu	Ireland
태국	taillaendeu	Thailand
인도네시아	indonesia	Indonesia
말레이시아	malleisia	Malaysia
인도	indo	India
싱가포르	singgaporeu	Singapore
필리핀	pillipin	Philippines
베트남	beteunam	Vietnam
브라질	beurajil	Brazil
러시아	reosia	Russia
실례합니다.	sillyehamnida	Excuse me.
고맙습니다.	gomapseumnida	Thank you.
감사합니다.	gamsahamnida	Thank you.
태극기	taegeukgi	Korean national flag
무궁화	mugunghwa	Rose of Sharon (Korean national flower)
아기	agi	baby
가방	gabang	bag

List of Words and Phrases

Unit 05 한국 사람이에요?

고양이	goyangi	cat
공	gong	ball
주스	juseu	juice
우유	uyu	milk
에드먼드 힐러리	edeumeondeu hilleori	Edmund Hillary
니콜 키드먼	nikol kideumeon	Nicole Kidman
마이클 조던	maikeul jodeon	Michael Jordan
질문하세요.	jilmunhaseyo	Please ask a question.
대답하세요.	daedaphaseyo	Please answer.

Unit 06 어디에 살아요?

어디	eodi	where
–에	e	in
살아요	sarayo	live
네덜란드	nedeollandeu	Netherlands
독일	dogil	Germany
프랑스	peurangseu	France
스페인	seupein	Spain
이탈리아	itallia	Italy
남아프리카공화국	namapeurika gonghwaguk	Republic of South Africa
서울	seoul	Seoul
시드니	sideuni	Sydney
도쿄	dokyo	Tokyo
밴쿠버	baenkubeo	Vancouver
오클랜드	okeullaendeu	Auckland
뉴욕	nyuyok	New York
런던	leondeon	London

Unit 06 어디에 살아요?

홍콩	hongkong	Hong Kong
알바니	albani	Albany
노스코트	noseucoteu	Northcote
노스크로스	noseukeuroseu	Northcross
켈스톤	kelseuton	Kelston
호랑이	horangi	tiger
호돌이	hodori	Hodori (the name of Seoul Olympic Games' mascot)
해리	haeri	Harry
타잔	tajan	Tarzan
정글	jeonggeul	jungle
개	gae	dog
개미	gaemi	ant
학교	hakgyo	school
해	hae	sun
카메라	kamera	camera
캥거루	kaenggeoru	kangaroo
앞으로 가세요.	apeuro gaseyo	Please go forward.
뒤로 가세요.	dwiro gaseyo	Please go backward.

Unit 07 피터 어디 있어요?

– 있어요	isseoyo	There is/are ~
– 없어요	eopseoyo	There is no ~
여기	yeogi	here
저기	jeogi	there
피터	piteo	Peter
피터팬	piteopaen	Peter Pan
교실	gyosil	classroom
수영장	suyeongjang	swimming pool
테니스장	teniseujang	tennis court
화장실	hwajangsil	rest room
도서관	doseogwan	library
운동장	undongjang	playing field/stadium
강당	gangdang	assembly hall
한옥	hanok	traditional Korean house
아파트	apateu	apartment
사과	sagwa	apple
전화기	jeonhwagi	telephone
택시	taeksi	taxi
텔레비전	tellebijeon	television
토마토	tomato	tomato
피아노	piano	piano
여기 보세요.	yeogi boseyo	Please look here.
저기 보세요.	jeogi boseyo	Please look there.

Unit 08 이게 뭐예요?

이게	ige	this
저게	jeoge	that
의자	uija	chair
책상	chaeksang	desk
칠판	chilpan	blackboard
컴퓨터	keompyuteo	computer
시계	sigye	clock/watch
책	chaek	book
지도	jido	map
문	mun	door
창문	changmun	window
맞아요.	majayo	(It is) right.
틀려요.	teullyeoyo	(It is) wrong.
한복	hanbok	traditional Korean costume
저고리	jeogori	traditional Korean jacket
바지	baji	pants
치마	chima	skirt
조끼	jokki	vest
버선	beoseon	traditional Korean socks
고무신	gomusin	traditional Korean rubber shoes
차	cha	car
치약	chiyak	toothpaste
치즈	chijeu	cheese
의사	uisa	doctor
펴세요.	pyeoseyo	Please open (the book).
덮으세요.	deopeuseyo	Please close (the book).

Unit 09 지우개 있어요?

지우개	jiugae	eraser
– 있어요	isseoyo	(I) have ~
– 없어요	eopseoyo	(I) do not have ~
종이	jongi	paper
공책	gongchaek	notebook
연필	yeonpil	pencil
필통	piltong	pencil case
자	ja	ruler
연필깎이	yeonpilkkaki	pencil sharpener
질문	jilmun	question
곶감	gotgam	dried persimmon
도깨비	dokkaebi	(Korean) goblin
뚝딱	ttukttak	thump
꼬리	kkori	tail
코끼리	kokkiri	elephant
땅콩	ttangkong	peanut
빵	ppang	bread
쓰레기통	sseuregitong	garbage bin / can
읽으세요.	ilgeuseyo	Please read.
쓰세요.	sseuseyo	Please write.
시작	sijak	start
끝	kkeut	end/finish

Unit 10 펜 좀 주세요.

펜	pen	pen
좀	jom	please, a little
주세요.	juseyo	Please give (it / them to me).
풀	pul	glue
색종이	saekjongi	colored paper
크레용	keureyong	crayon
휴지	hyuji	tissue / toilet paper
천만에요.	cheonmaneyo	Not at all. / You're welcome.
미안해요.	mianhaeyo	I'm sorry.
괜찮아요.	gwaenchanayo	That's alright. / It's okay.
오리	ori	duck
새	sae	bird
돼지	dwaeji	pig
키위	kiwi	kiwi
펭귄	penggwin	penguin
꽥꽥	kkwaek-kkwaek	quack-quack
짹짹	jjaek-jjaek	chirp-chirp
꿀꿀	kkul-kkul	oink-oink
나	na	I (casual form)
깔깔	kkal-kkal	ha-ha
시작하세요.	sijakhaseyo	Please start.
그만하세요.	geumanhaseyo	Please stop.
탈춤	talchum	(Korean) mask dance

The Sounds of the Korean Alphabet

Fourteen basic consonant letters

letter	sounds similar to the bold letter	can be written as
ㄱ	**g**oose	g, k ^
ㄴ	**n**ose	n
ㄷ	**d**inosaur	d, t ^
ㄹ	**r**ibbon / fee**l**	r, l ^^
ㅁ	**m**oney	m
ㅂ	**b**ucket	b, p ^
ㅅ	**s**nake	s
ㅇ	ri**ng***	ng
ㅈ	**j**azz	j
ㅊ	**ch**urch	ch
ㅋ	**k**ey	k
ㅌ	**t**elephone	t
ㅍ	**p**ot	p
ㅎ	**h**at	h

Other consonant letters

letter	sounds similar to the bold letter	can be written as
ㄲ	**sk**in	kk
ㄸ	s**t**ill	tt
ㅃ	s**p**in	pp
ㅆ	**s**and	ss
ㅉ	pi**zz**a	jj

* Before a vowel, ㅇ does not make any sound. In the final position after a vowel, however, it sounds like the last part of "si**ng**" or "so**ng**."

^ Before a vowel or between vowels, ㄱ, ㄷ and ㅂ are written as "g, d and b." Before a consonant, they are usually written as "k, t and p." At the end of a word, they are always written as "k, t and p."

^^ Before a vowel or between vowels, ㄹ is written as "r." Before a consonant or at the end of a word, ㄹ is written as "l." ㄹㄹ is written as "ll."

Ten basic vowel letters

letter	sounds similar to the bold letter	can be written as
ㅏ	**fa**ther	a
ㅑ	**ya**hoo	ya
ㅓ	**a**go	eo
ㅕ	**you**ng	yeo
ㅗ	**o**pen	o
ㅛ	**yo**ga	yo
ㅜ	**soo**n	u
ㅠ	**you**	yu
ㅡ	**pu**ll *	eu
ㅣ	**fee**t	i

Other vowel letters

letter	sounds similar to the bold letter	can be written as
ㅐ	**ca**t	ae
ㅒ	**Ya**nkee	yae
ㅔ	**pe**n	e
ㅖ	**ye**s	ye
ㅘ	Ha**wa**ii	wa
ㅙ	**wa**x	wae
ㅚ	**we**t	oe
ㅝ	**wa**ter	wo
ㅞ	**we**t	we
ㅟ	**we**	wi
ㅢ	**	ui

* No lip rounding.

** No matching sound in English. Say ㅡ and ㅣ quickly one after the other.